HARMENSZ REMBRANDT

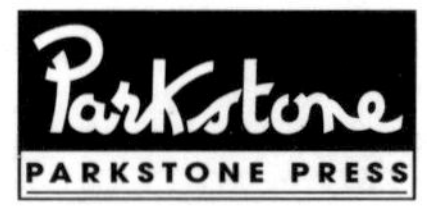

Printed in Europe
ISBN 1 85995 429 4
© Parkstone Publishers, Bournemouth, 1997

HARMENSZ REMBRANDT
(1606-1669)

A Rembrandt picture is a live entity existing according to its own laws,
reflecting the multitude of thoughts and emotions present in the painter's mind.
Man and his state of mind - this is the fundamental problem which engages the
artist his whole life long. Troubled by family problems, he took refuge in painting,
which became steadily more sumptuous as things got worse, as if painted
by a visionary. By masking his distress under the optimism of his subjects
and the strength of his sombre colours he emerged victorious.

HARMENSZ REMBRANDT
(1606-1669)

Un tableau de Rembrandt est une entité vivant selon ses propres lois,
reflétant la multitude d'émotions et de pensées du peintre. L'Homme et son état
d'âme, voilà le problème fondamental qui préoccupera l'artiste durant
toute sa vie et chacune de ses oeuvres en est la vive expression.
Accablé par les drames familiaux, il se réfugie dans la peinture qui devient
alors plus somptueuse, comme exécutée par un visionnaire. C'est en masquant
sa détresse sous l'optimisme de ses sujets, sous la splendeur de ses tons
que Rembrandt sortira victorieux.

HARMENSZ REMBRANDT
(1606-1669)

Ein Gemälde von Rembrandt ist ein lebendiges Ganzes, das seinen eigenen
Gesetzen folgt und die Vielzahl von Gefühlen und Gedanken des Malers
widerspiegelt. Der Mensch und sein seelisches Befinden ist das Grundthema,
das den Künstler sein ganzes Leben lang beschäftigen wird und das in jedem
seiner Gemälde anschaulich zum Ausdruck kommt.
Von Familientragödien verfolgt, flüchtet er sich in die Malerei,
deren visionäre Kraft sich immer mehr steigert. Indem er sein eigenes tragisches
Schicksal hinter dem Optimismus seiner Sujets verbirgt,
vollendet Rembrandt seine künstlerische Laufbahn.

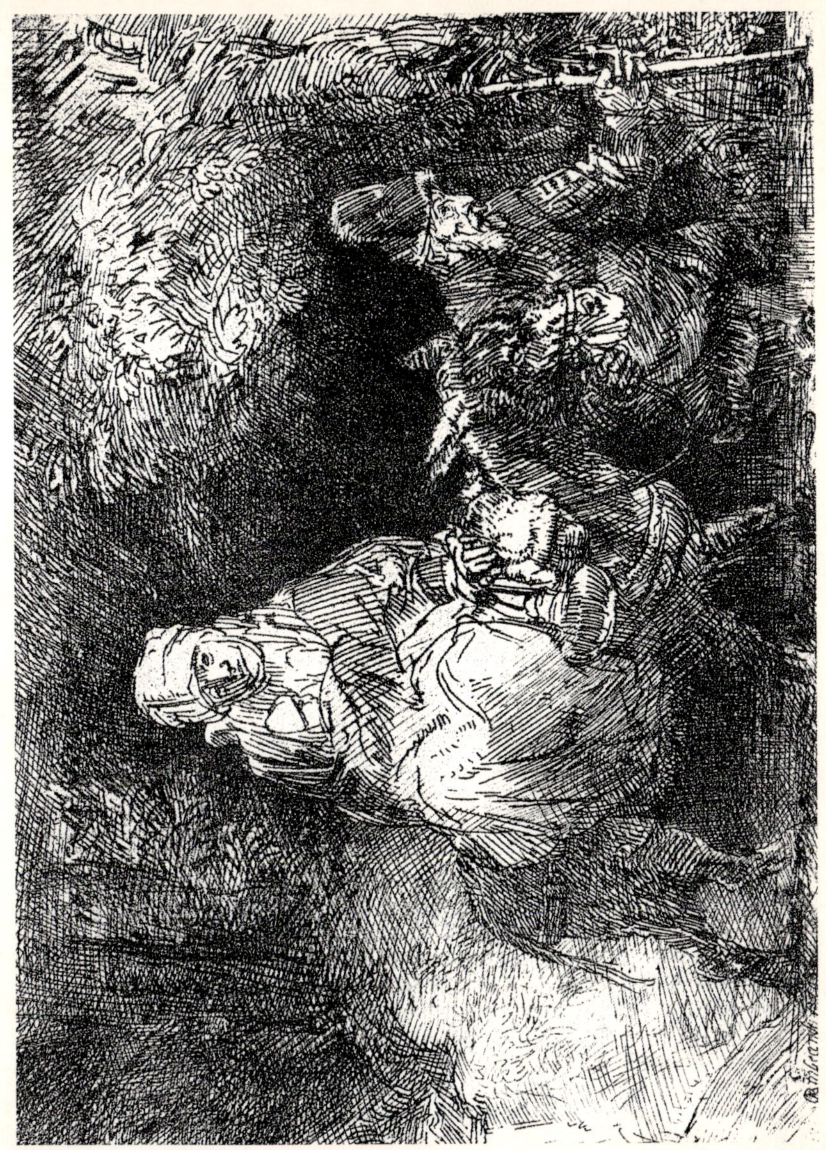

THE FLIGHT INTO EGYPT : CROSSING A
BROOK, 1654

LA FUITE EN EGYPTE : TRAVERSEE D'UN
RUISSEAU, 1654

DIE FLUCHT NACH ÄGYPTEN :
DURCHSCHREINTEN BACHES, 1654

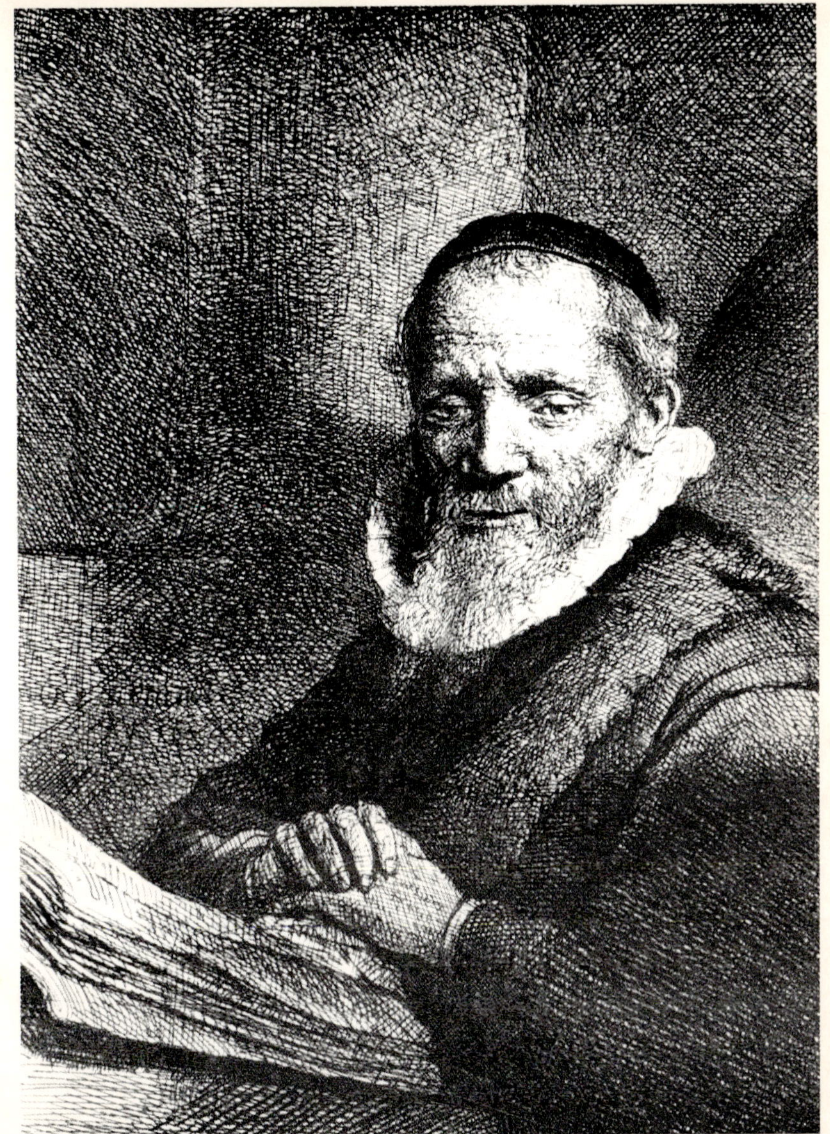

PORTRAIT OF JAN CORNELIS SYLVIUS,
PREACHER, 1633

PORTRAIT DU PASTEUR JAN CORNELISZ
SYLVIUS, 1633

BILDNIS DES PREDIGERS JAN CORNELISZ
SYLVIUS, 1633

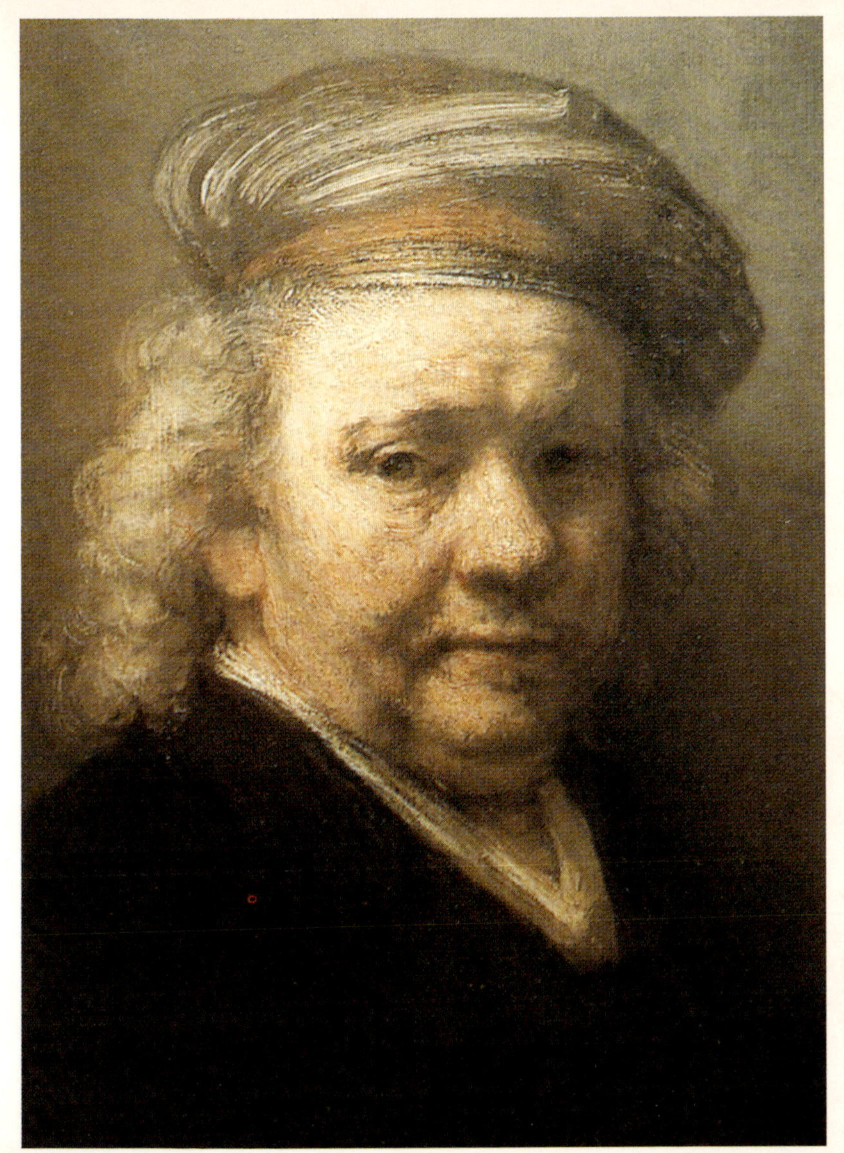

SELF-PORTRAIT, 1669
Mauritshuis, The Hague

AUTOPORTRAIT, 1669
Mauritshuis, La Haye

AUTOPORTRAIT, 1669
Mauritshuis, La Haye

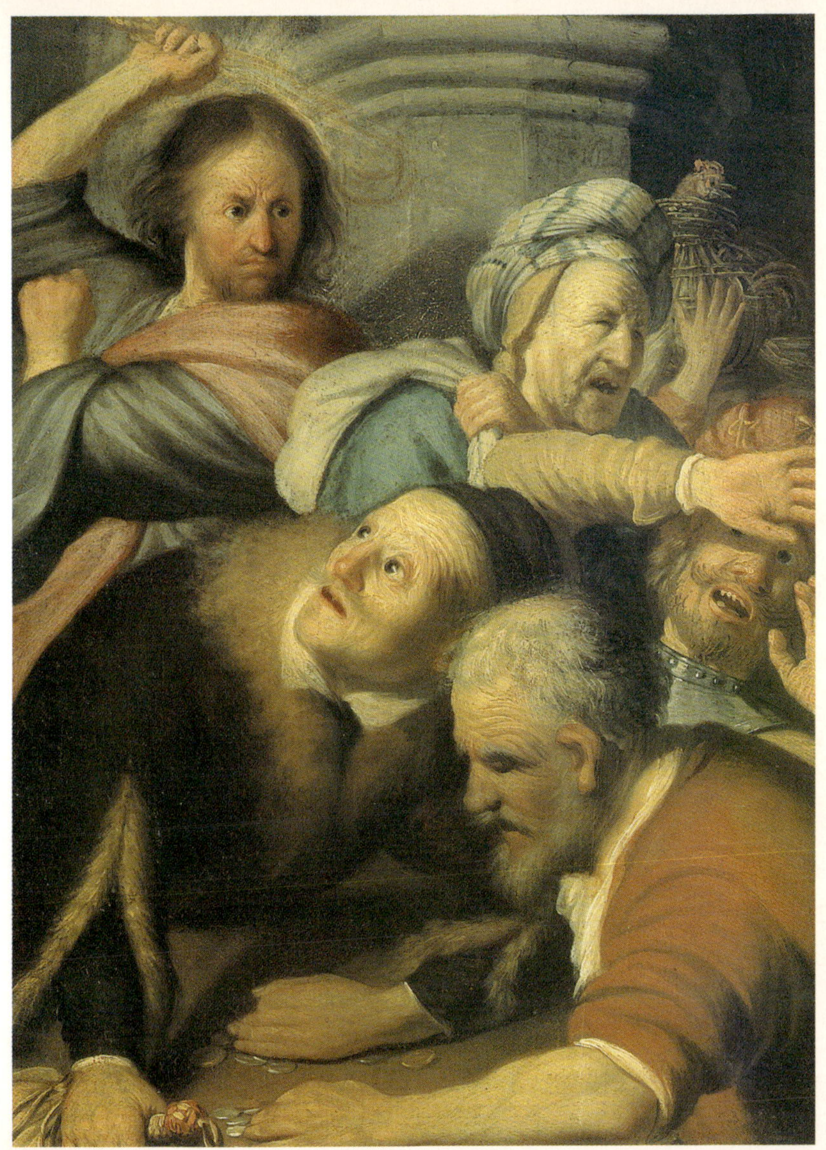

CHRIST DRIVING THE MONEY - CHANGERS
FROM THE TEMPLE (Detail), 1626
Oil on wood (oak). 43 x 33 cm
Moscow, Pushkin Museum

LE CHRIST CHASSANT LES MARCHANDS DU
TEMPLE (Détail), 1626
Huile sur bois (chêne). 43 x 33 cm
Moscou, Musée des Beaux Arts Pouchkine

DIE TEMPELREINIGUNG (Detail), 1626
Öl auf Holz (eiche). 43 x 33 cm
Moskau, Kunstmuseum Puschkin

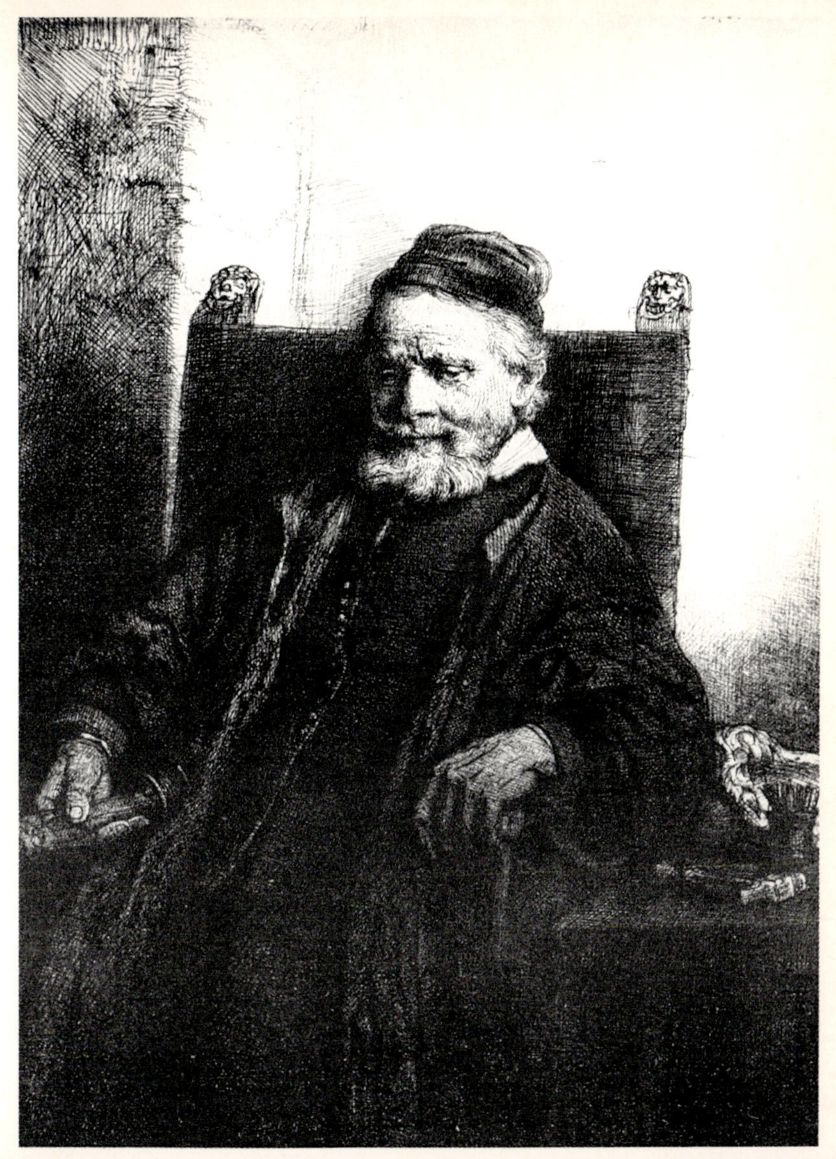

JAN LUTMA THE ELMER, GOLDSMITH

PORTRAIT DE L'ORFEVRE JAN LUTMA L'ANCIEN

DER GOLDSCHMIED JAN LUTMA DER ÄLTERE

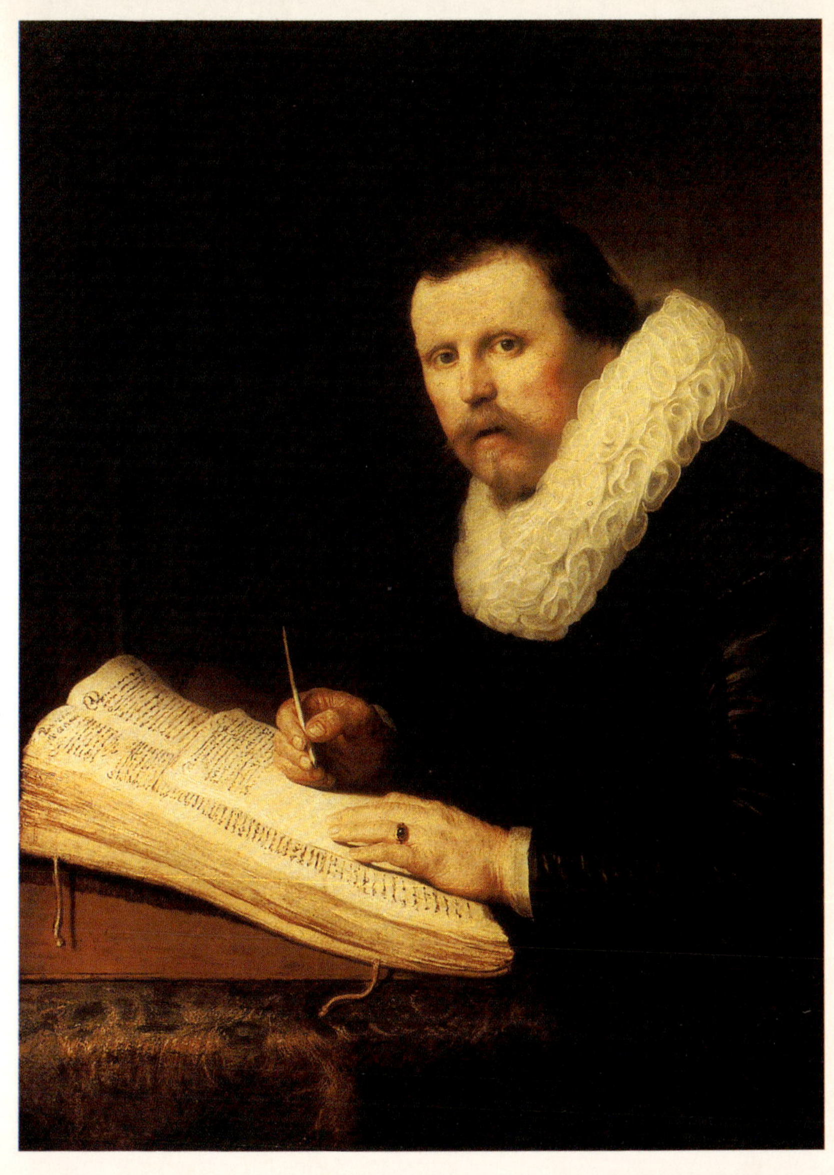

PORTRAIT OF AN OLD MAN, 1631
Oil on canvas. 104,5 x 92 cm
St. Petersburg, Hermitage Museum

PORTRAIT DE SAVANT, 1631
Huile sur toile. 104,5 x 92 cm
Saint-Pétersbourg, Musée de l'Ermitage

BILDNIS EINES WISSENSCHAFTLERS, 1631
Öl auf Leinand. 104,5 x 92 cm
St. Petersburg, Ermitage

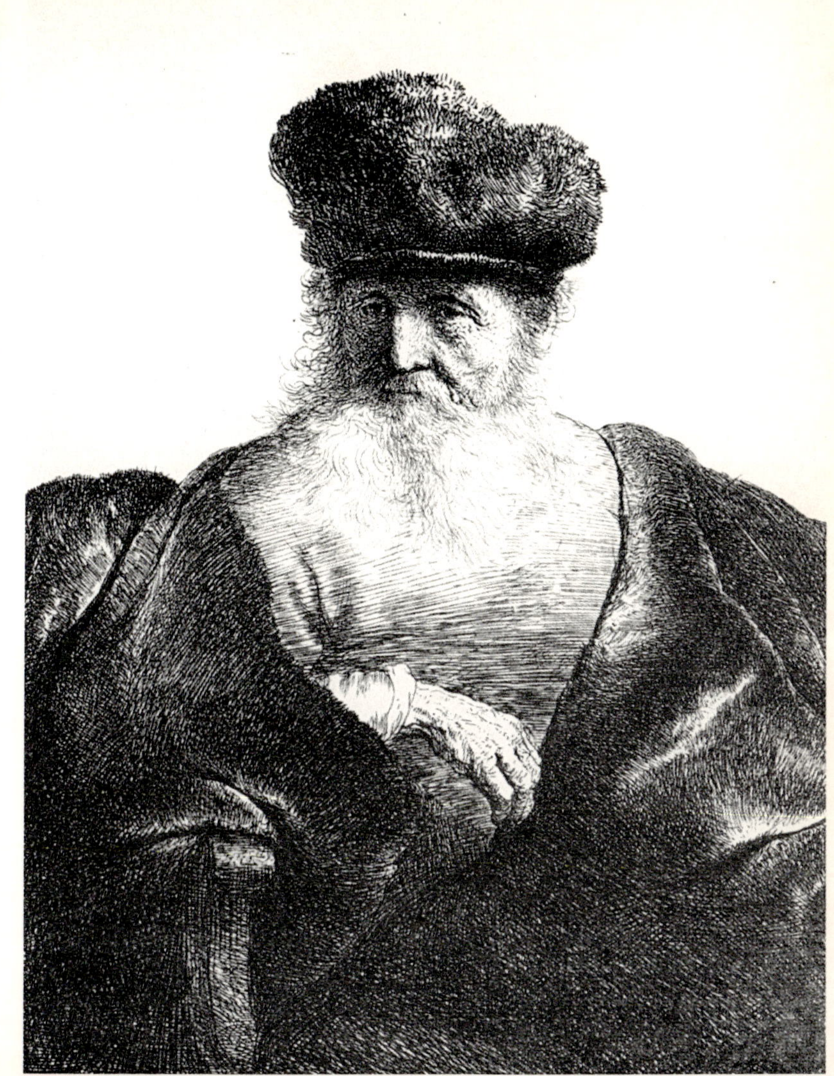

OLD MAN WITH BEARD, FUR CAP AND
VELVET CLOARK

FIGURE DE VIEILLARD AU BONNET DE
FOURRURE ET AU MANTEAU DE VELOURS

ALTER MANN MIT PELZMÜTZE UND
SAMTMANTEL

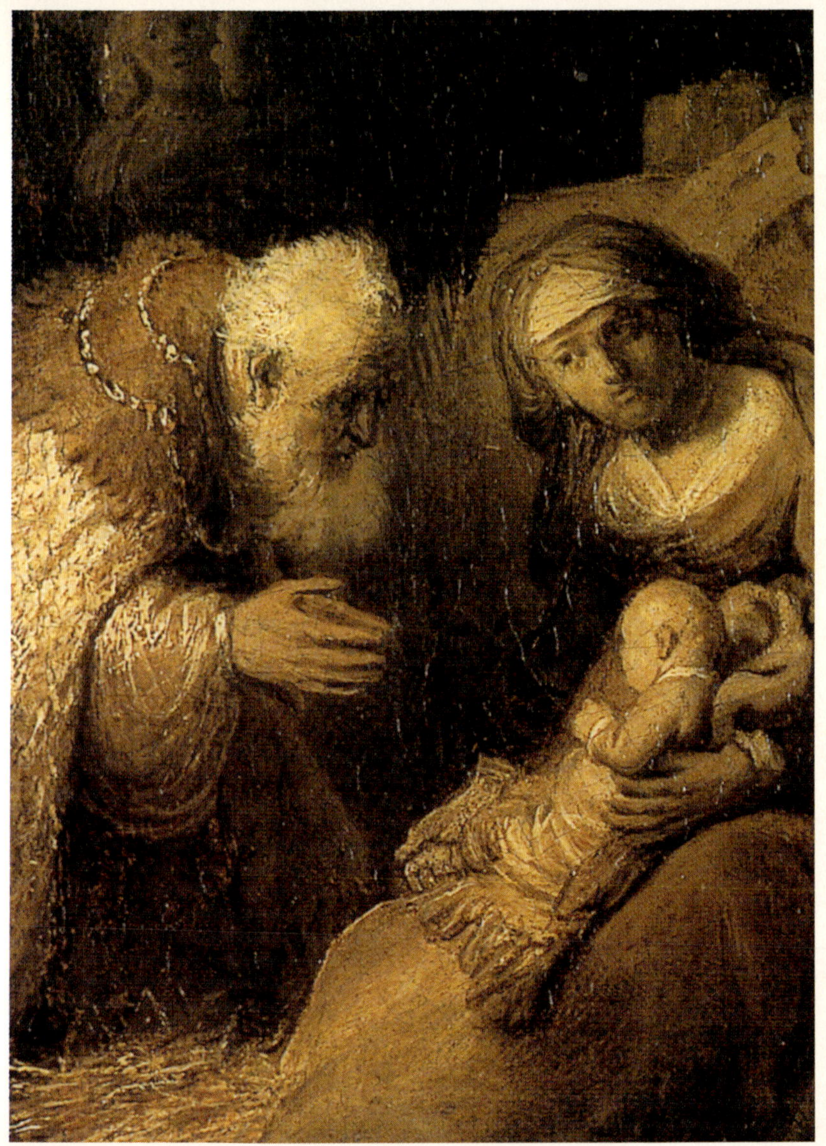

THE ADORATION OF THE MAGI (Detail), 1632
Oil on paper glued to canvas. 45 x 39 cm
St. Petersburg, Hermitage Museum

L'ADORATION DES MAGES (Détail), 1632
Huile sur papier collé sur toile. 45 x 39 cm
Saint-Pétersbourg, Musée de l'Ermitage

ANBETUNG DER KÖNIGE (Detail), 1632
Öl auf Papier, auf Leinand aufgeklebt. 45 x 39 cm
St. Petersburg, Ermitage

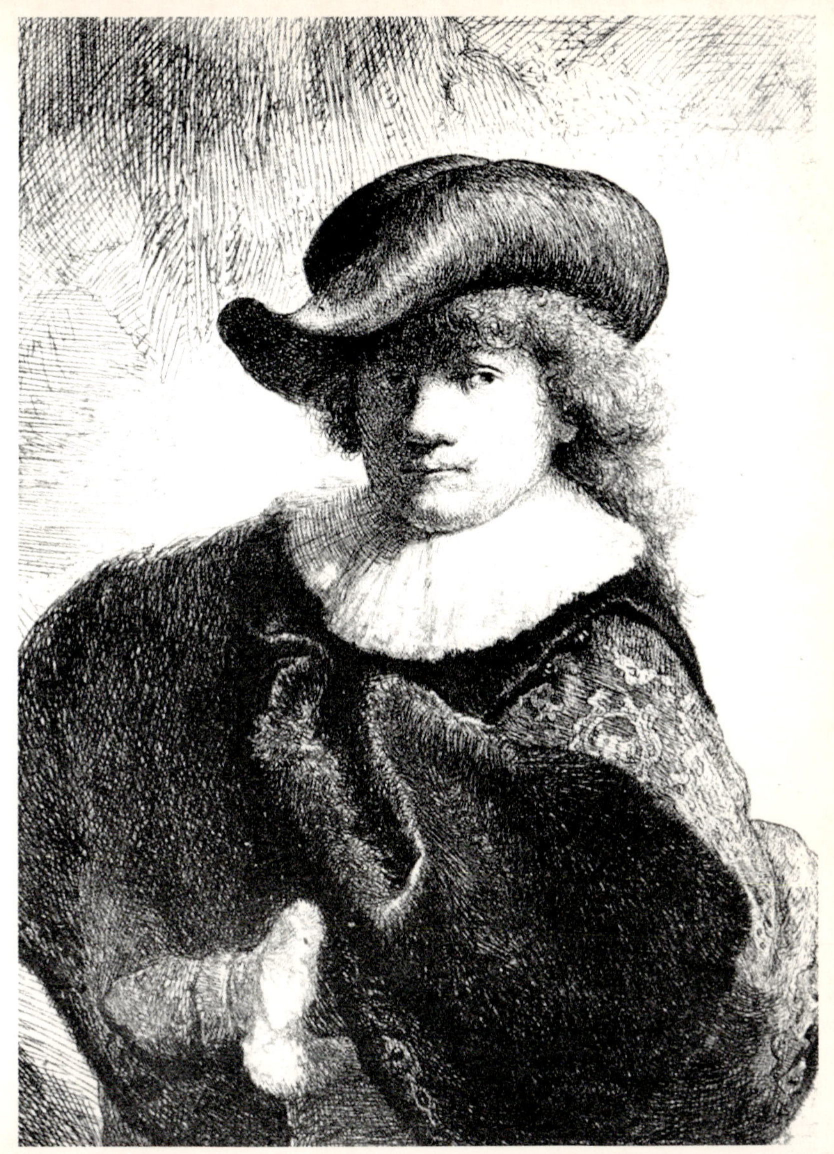

REMBRANDT IN A SOFT HAT AND EMBROIDE-
RED CLOAK

AUTOPORTRAIT AU CHAPEAU ROND ET AU
MANTEAU BRODE

SELBSBILDNIS MIT RUNDEM HUT UND
BESTICKEM MANTEL

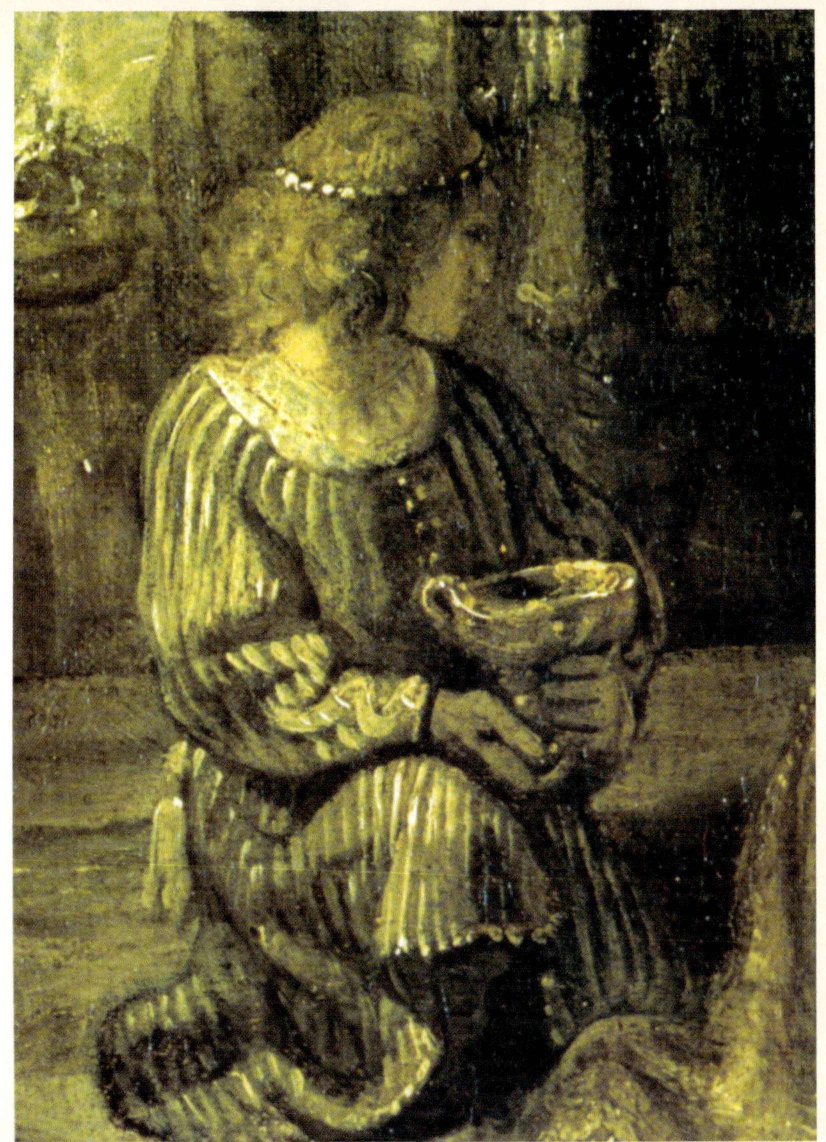

THE ADORATION OF THE MAGI (Detail), 1632
Oil on paper glued to canvas. 45 x 39 cm
St. Petersburg, Hermitage Museum

L'ADORATION DES MAGES (Détail), 1632
Huile sur papier collé sur toile. 45 x 39 cm
Saint-Pétersbourg, Musée de l'Ermitage

ANBETUNG DER KÖNIGE (Detail), 1632
Öl auf Papier, auf Leinand aufgeklebt. 45 x 39 cm
St. Petersburg, Ermitage

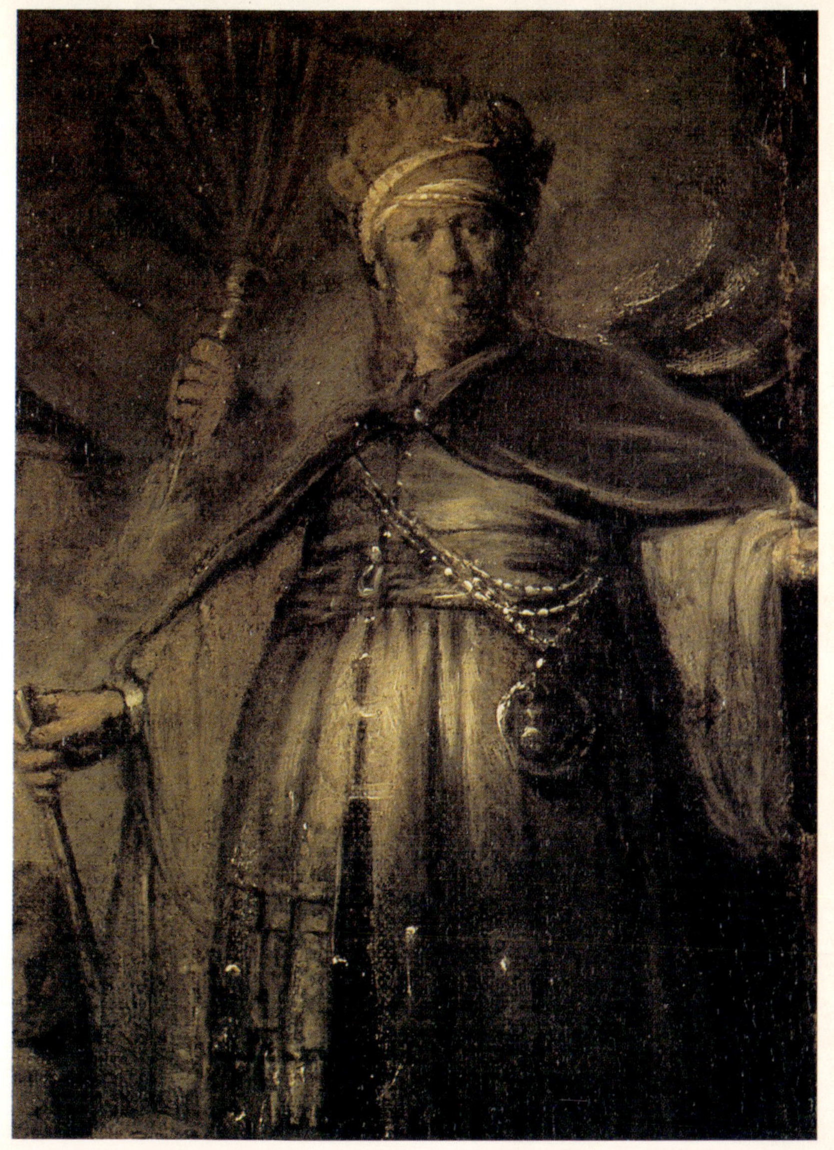

THE ADORATION OF THE MAGI (Detail), 1632
Oil on paper glued to canvas. 45 x 39 cm
St. Petersburg, Hermitage Museum

L'ADORATION DES MAGES (Détail), 1632
Huile sur papier collé sur toile. 45 x 39 cm
Saint-Pétersbourg, Musée de l'Ermitage

ANBETUNG DER KÖNIGE (Detail), 1632
Öl auf Papier, auf Leinand aufgeklebt. 45 x 39 cm
St. Petersburg, Ermitage

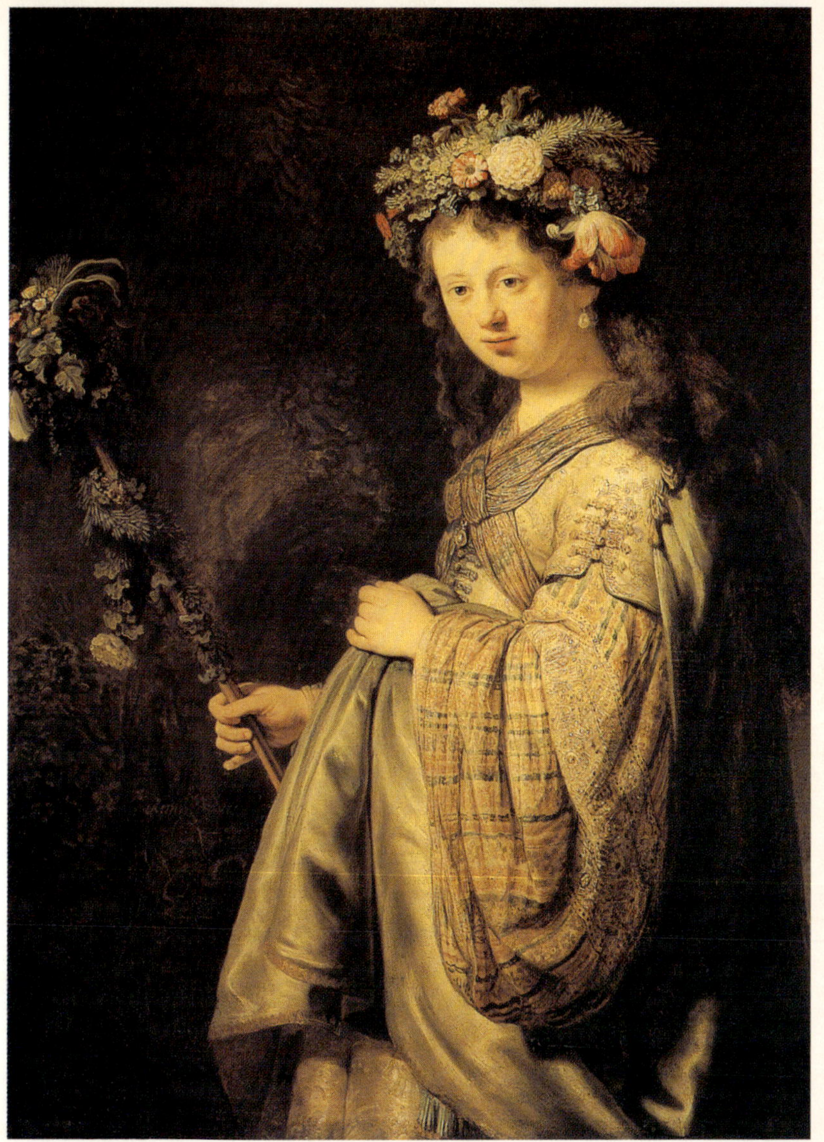

FLORE, 1634
Oil on canvas. 125 x 201 cm
St. Petersburg, Hermitage Museum

FLORE, 1634
Huile sur toile. 125 x 201 cm
Saint-Pétersbourg, Musée de l'Ermitage

FLORA, 1634
Öl auf Leinwand. 125 x 201 cm
St. Petersburg, Ermitage

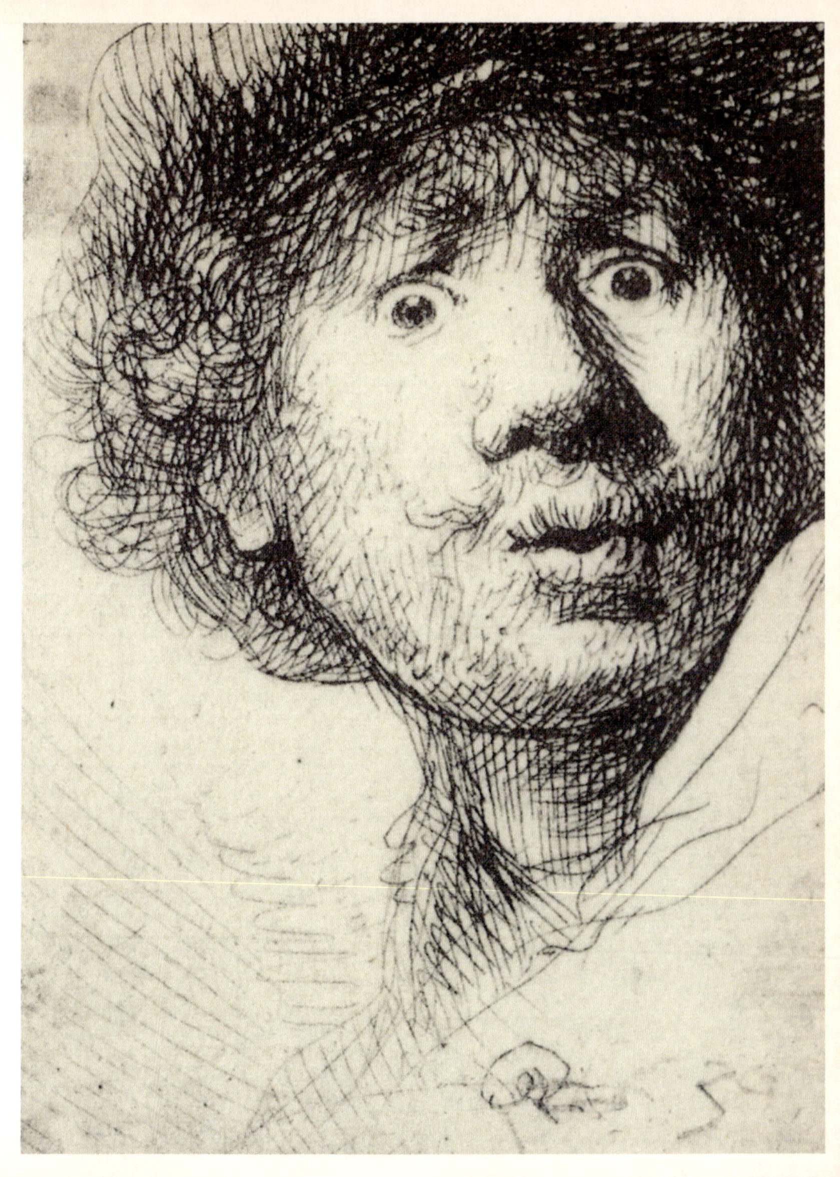

SELF-PORTRAIT IN A CAP, OPEN-MOUTHED, 1630

AUTOPORTRAIT A LA BOUCHE OUVERTE, 1630

SELBSTBILDNIS MIT OFFENEM MUND, 1630

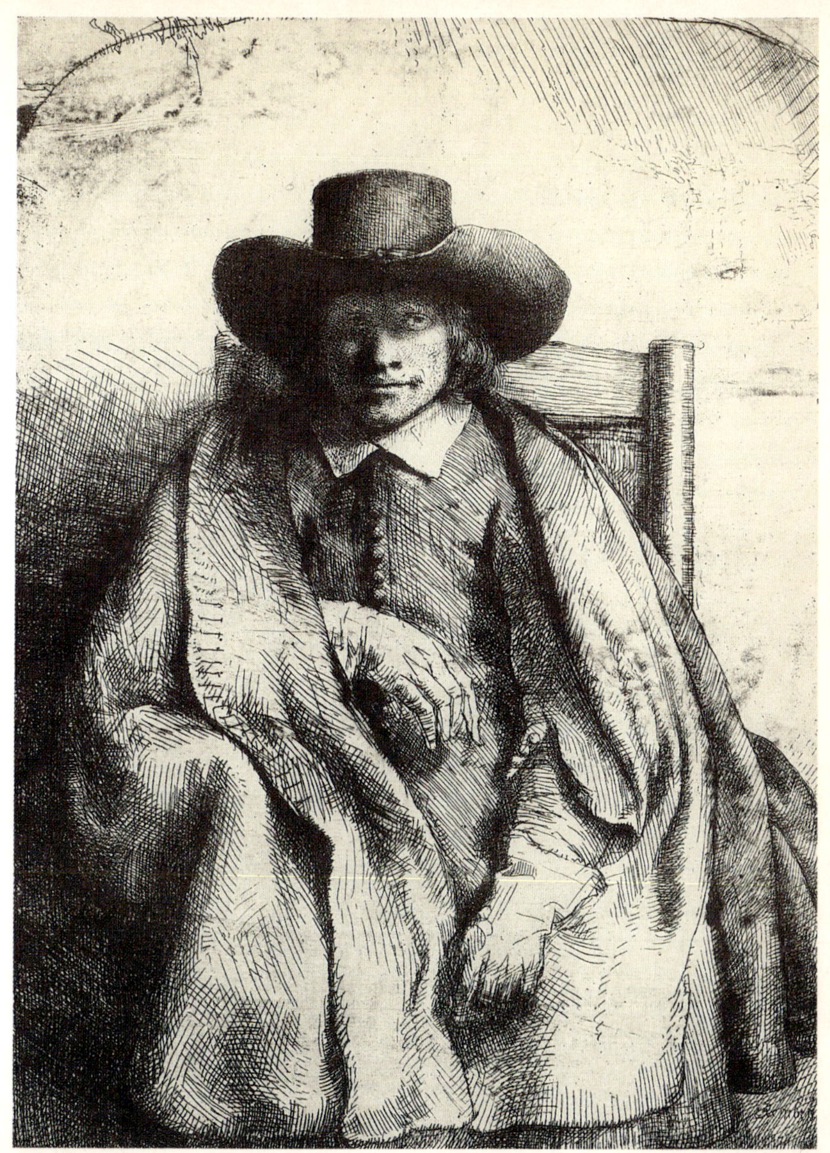

PORTRAIT OF CLEMENT DE JONGHE,
PUBLISHER OF PRINTS AND PRINTSELLER, 1651

PORTRAIT DE L'EDITEUR ET MARCHAND
D'ESTAMPES, CLEMENT DE JONGHE, 1651

BILDNIS DES KUNSTHÄNDLERS
CLEMENT DE JONGHE, 1651

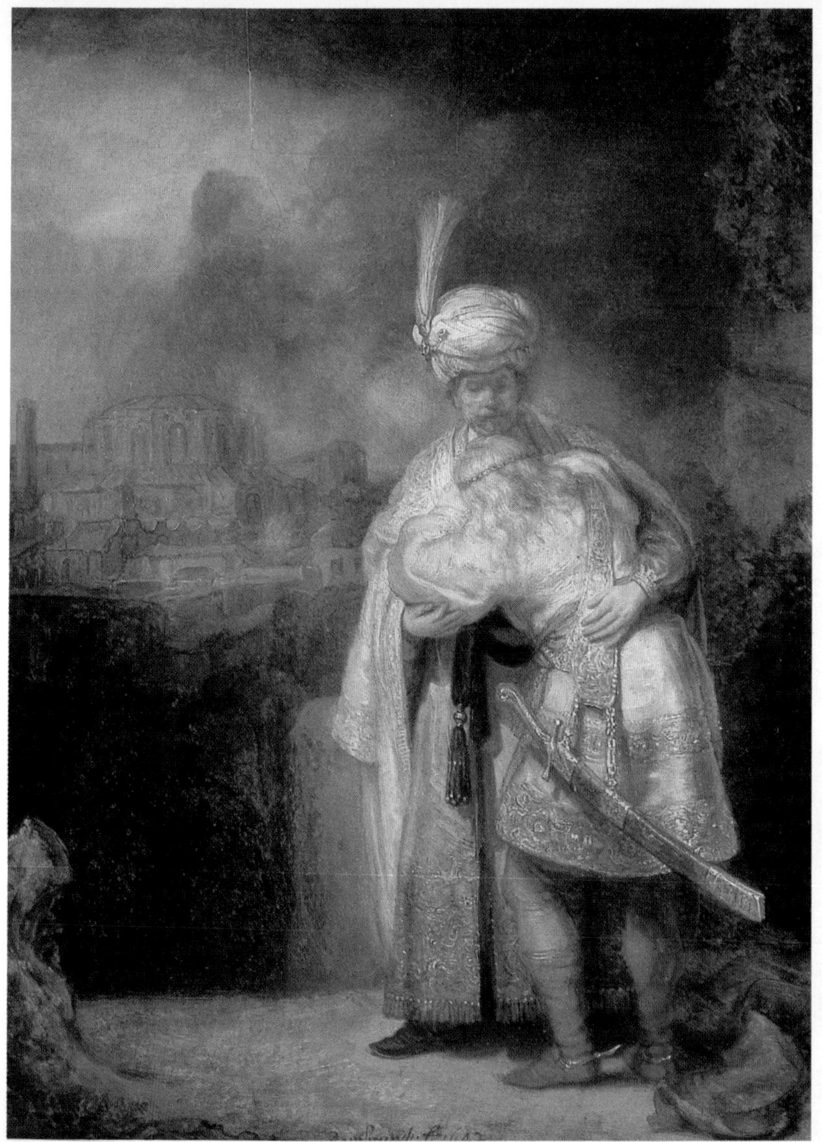

DAVID AND JONATHAN, 1642
Oil on wood. 73 x 61,5 cm
St. Petersburg, Hermitage Museum

DAVID ET JONATHAN, 1642
Huile sur bois. 73 x 61,5 cm
Saint-Pétersbourg, Musée de l'Ermitage

DAVID UND JONATHAN, 1642
Öl auf Holz. 73 x 61,5 cm
St. Petersburg, Ermitage

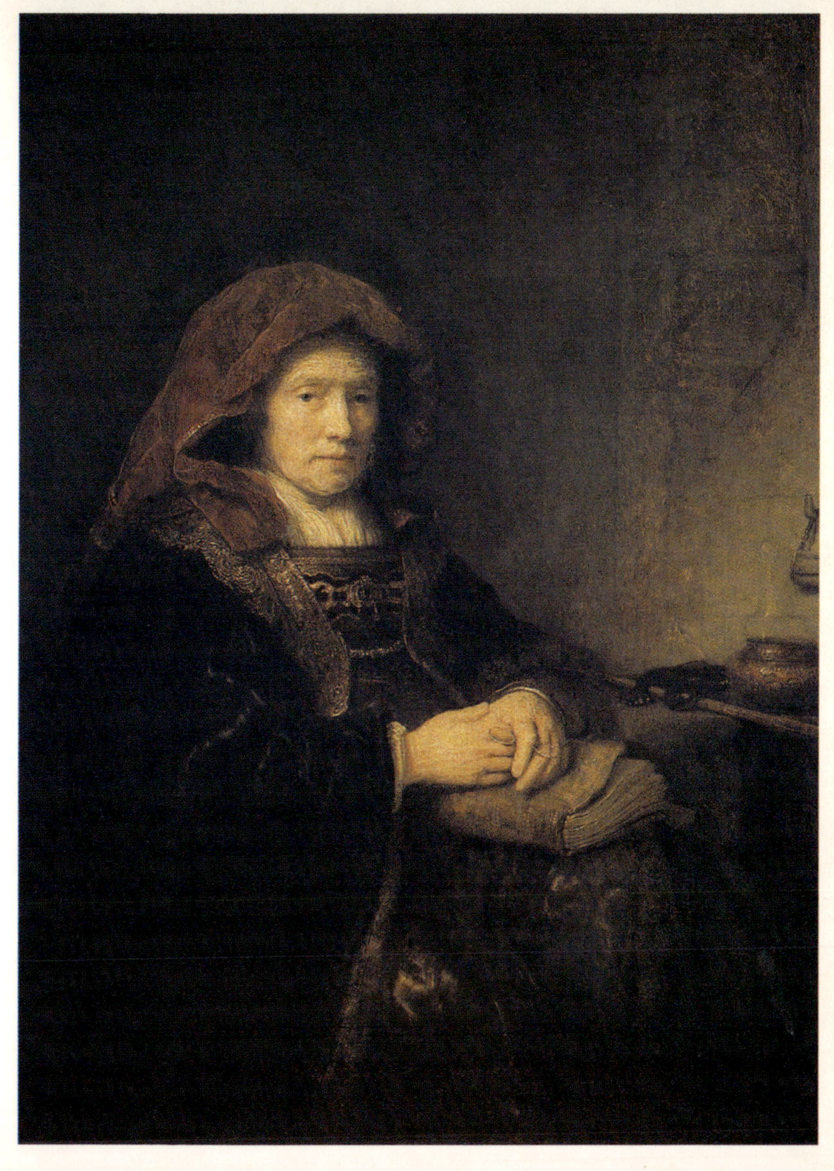

AN OLD WOMAN IN AN ARMCHAIR, 1643
Oil on wood. 61 x 49 cm
St. Petersburg, Hermitage Museum

PORTRAIT DE VIEILLE FEMME AUX BESICLES, 1643
Huile sur bois. 61 x 49 cm
Saint-Pétersbourg, Musée de l'Ermitage

BILDNIS EINER ALTEN FRAU MIT BRILLE, 1643
Öl auf Holz. 61 x 49 cm
St. Petersburg, Ermitage

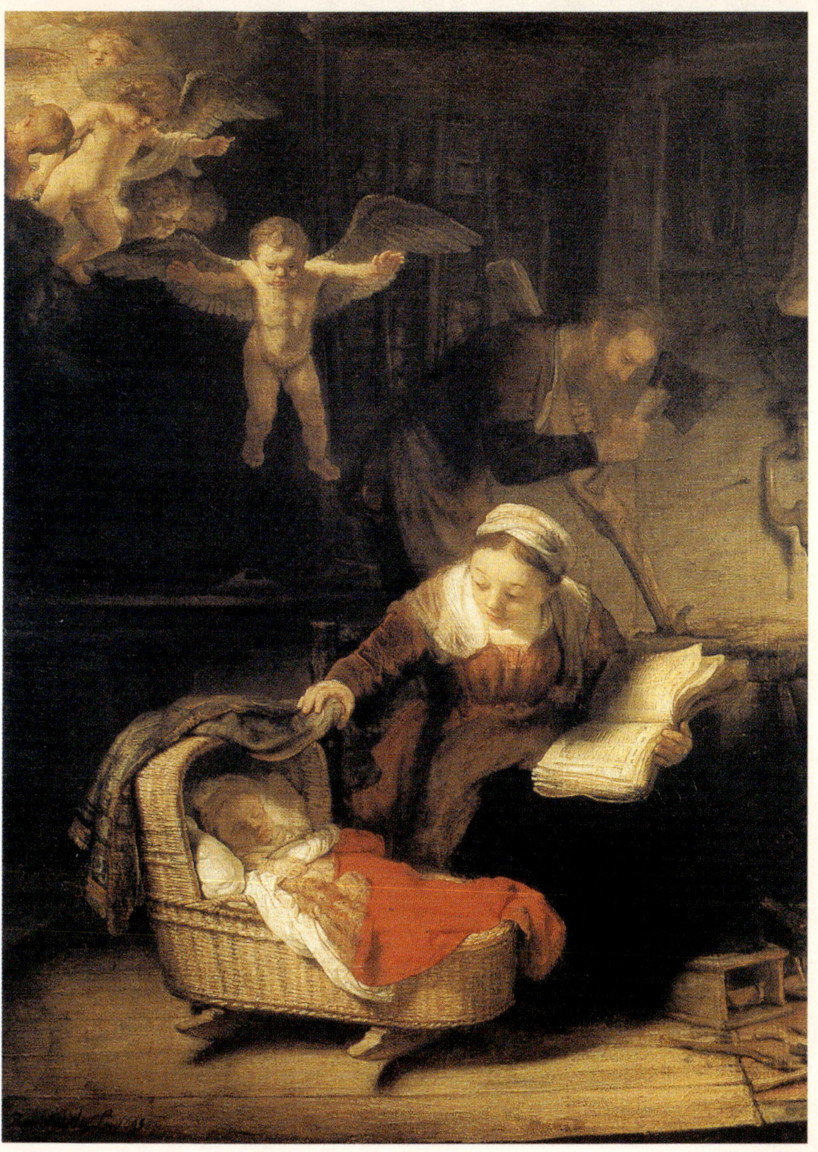

THE HOLY FAMILY WITH ANGELS, 1645
Oil on canvas. 117 x 91 cm
St. Petersburg, Hermitage Museum

LA SAINTE FAMILLE, 1645
Huile sur toile. 117 x 91 cm
Saint-Pétersbourg, Musée de l'Ermitage

DIE HEILIGE FAMILIE, 1645
Öl auf Leinand. 117 x 91 cm
St. Petersburg, Ermitage

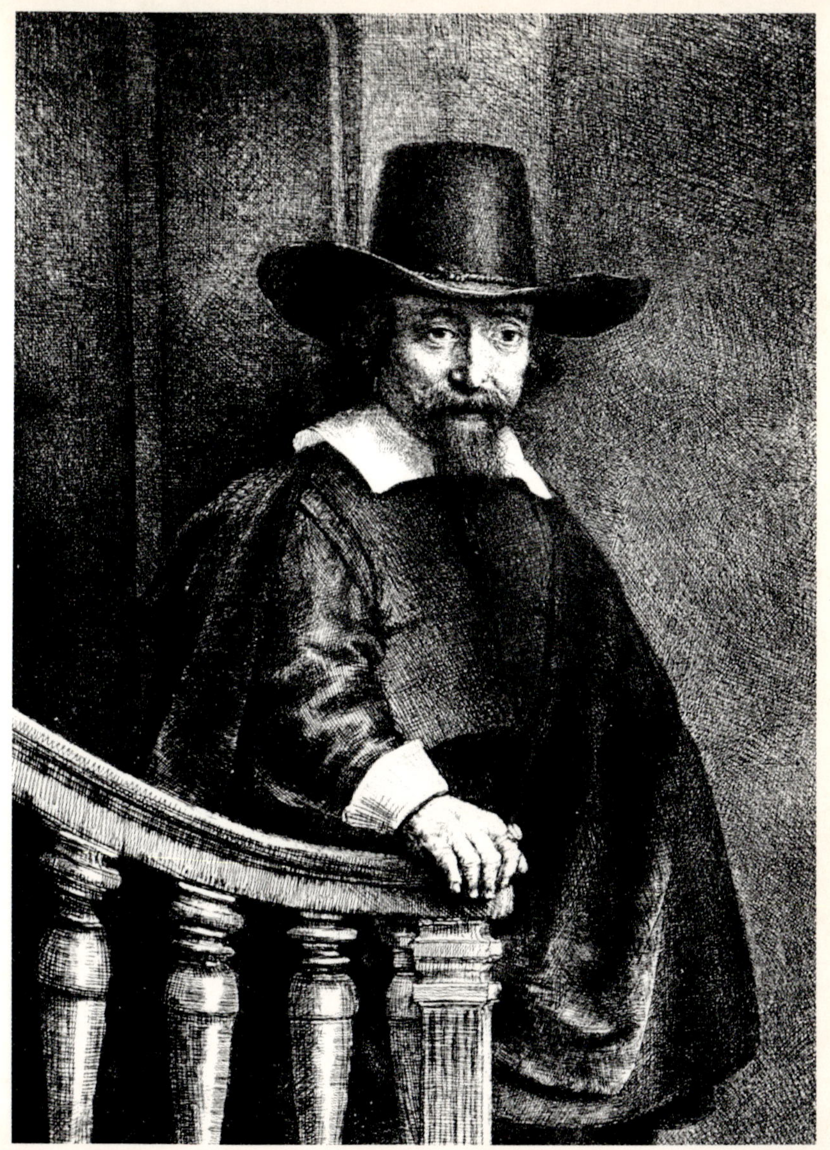

EPHRAÏM BUENO, JEWISH PHYSICIAN, 1647

PORTRAIT DU MEDECIN JUIF, EPHRAÏM
BUENO, 1647

BILDNIS DER JÜDISCHEN ARZTES EPHRAIM
BUENO, 1647

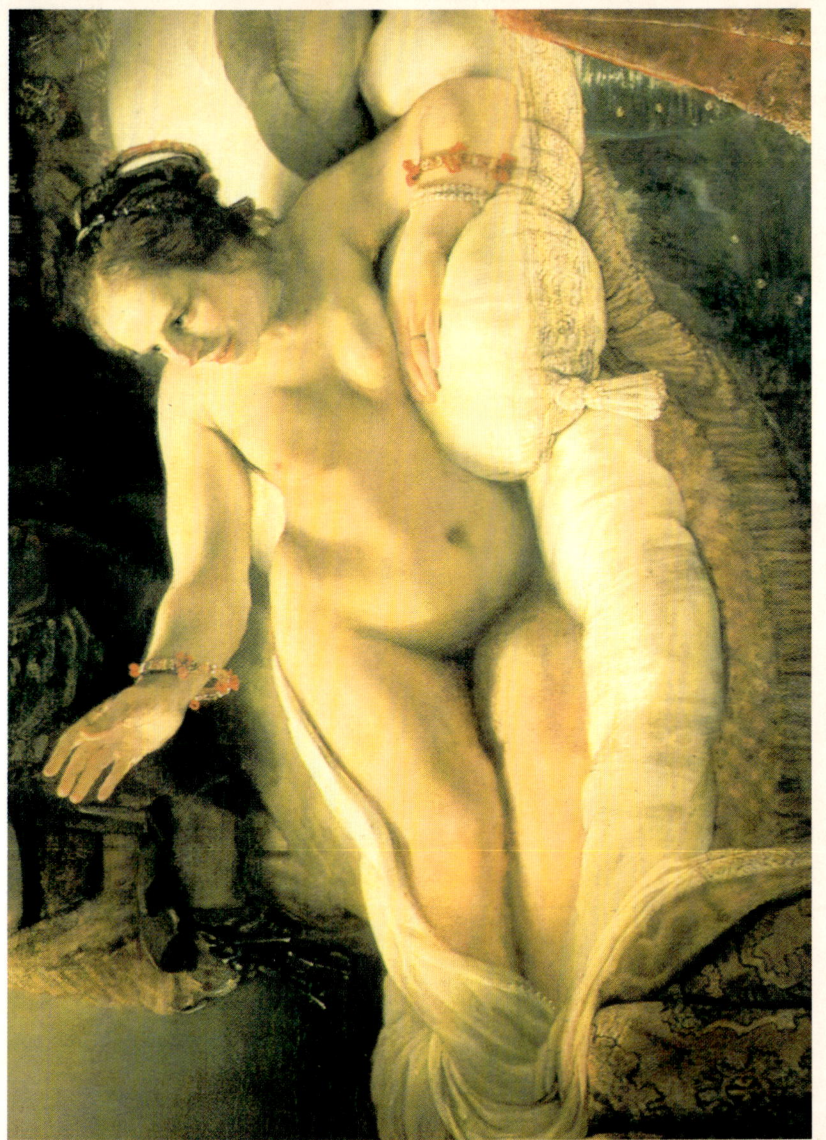

DANAE (Detail)
Oil on canvas. 185 x 203 cm
St. Petersburg, Hermitage Museum

DANAE (Détail)
Huile sur toile. 185 x 203 cm
Saint-Pétersbourg, Musée de l'Ermitage

DANAË (Detail)
Öl auf Leinwand. 185 x 203 cm
St. Petersburg, Ermitage

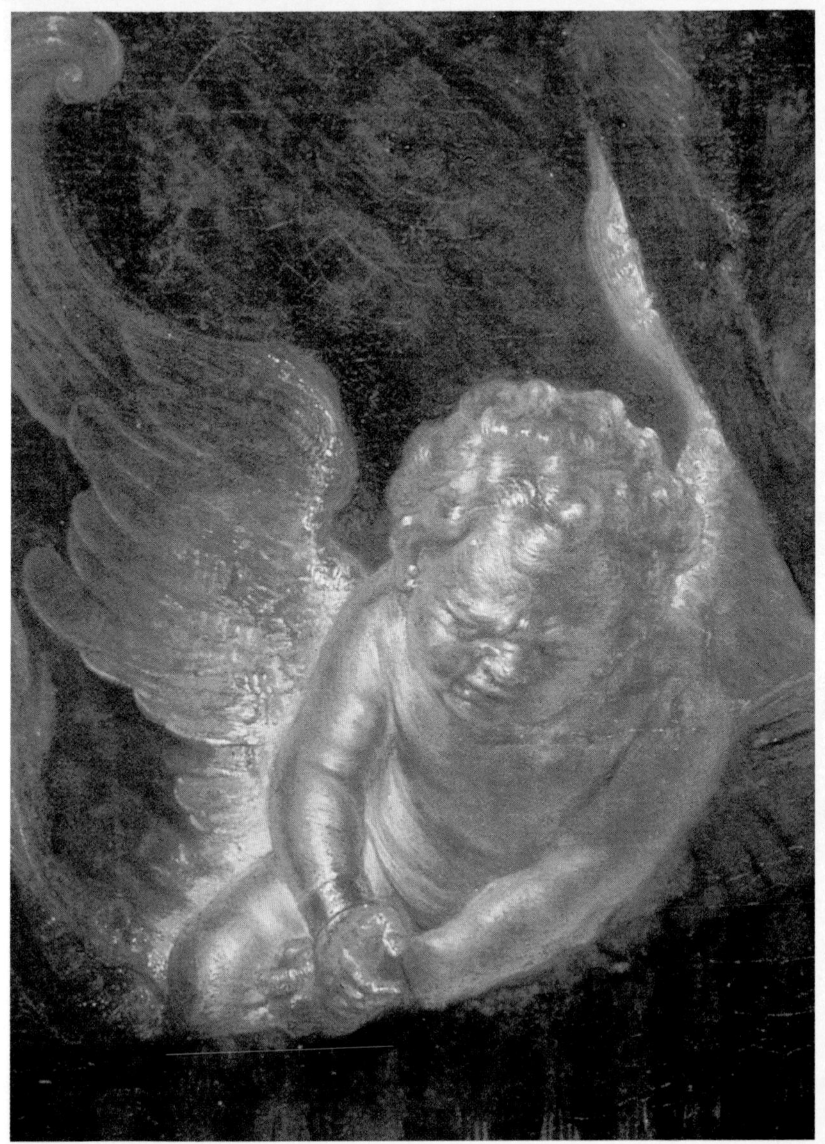

DANAE (Detail)
Oil on canvas. 185 x 203 cm
St Petersburg, Hermitage Museum

DANAE (Détail)
Huile sur toile. 185 x 203 cm
Saint-Pétersbourg, Musée de l'Ermitage

DANAË (Detail)
Öl auf Leinwand. 185 x 203 cm
St. Petersburg, Ermitage

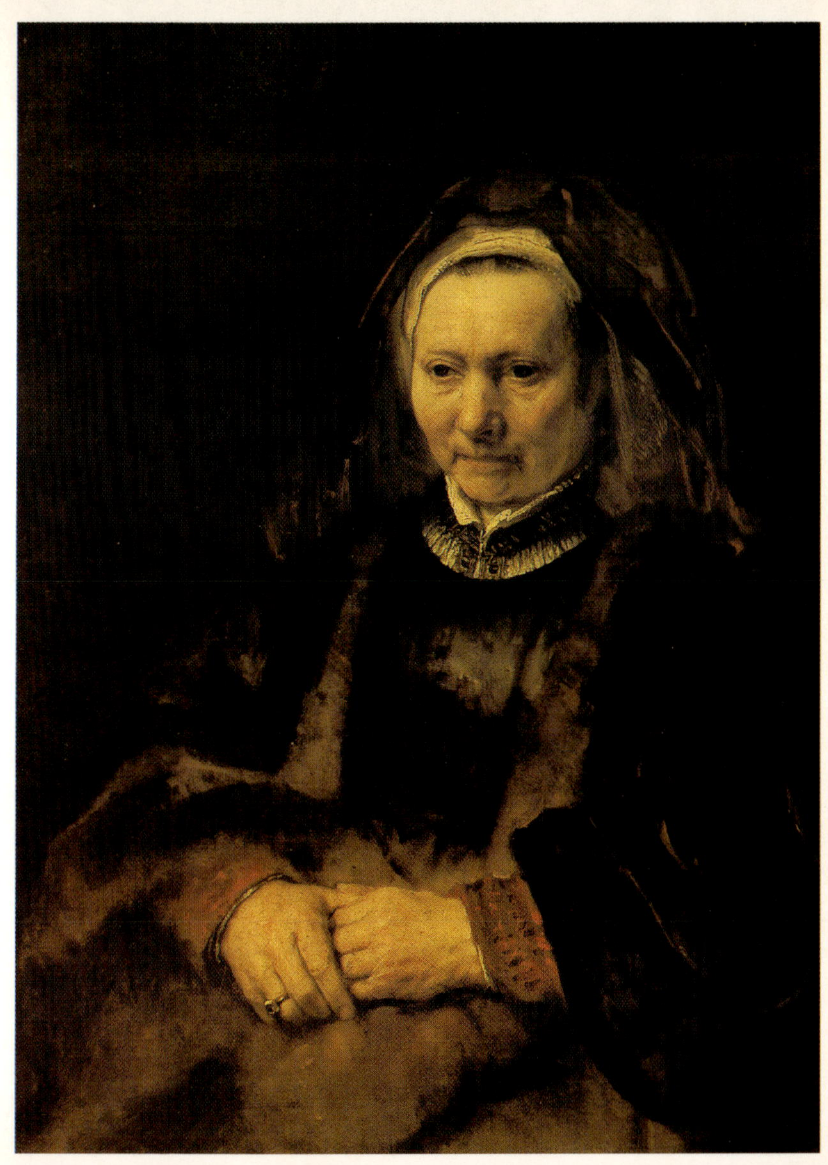

PORTRAIT OF AN OLD LADY
Oil on canvas. 82 x 72 cm
Moscow, Pushkin Museum

PORTRAIT DE FEMME AGEE
Huile sur toile. 82 x 72 cm
Moscou, Musée des Beaux Arts Pouchkine

BILDNIS EINER ALTEN FRAU
Öl auf Leinwand. 82 x 72 cm
Moskau, Kunstmuseum Puschkin

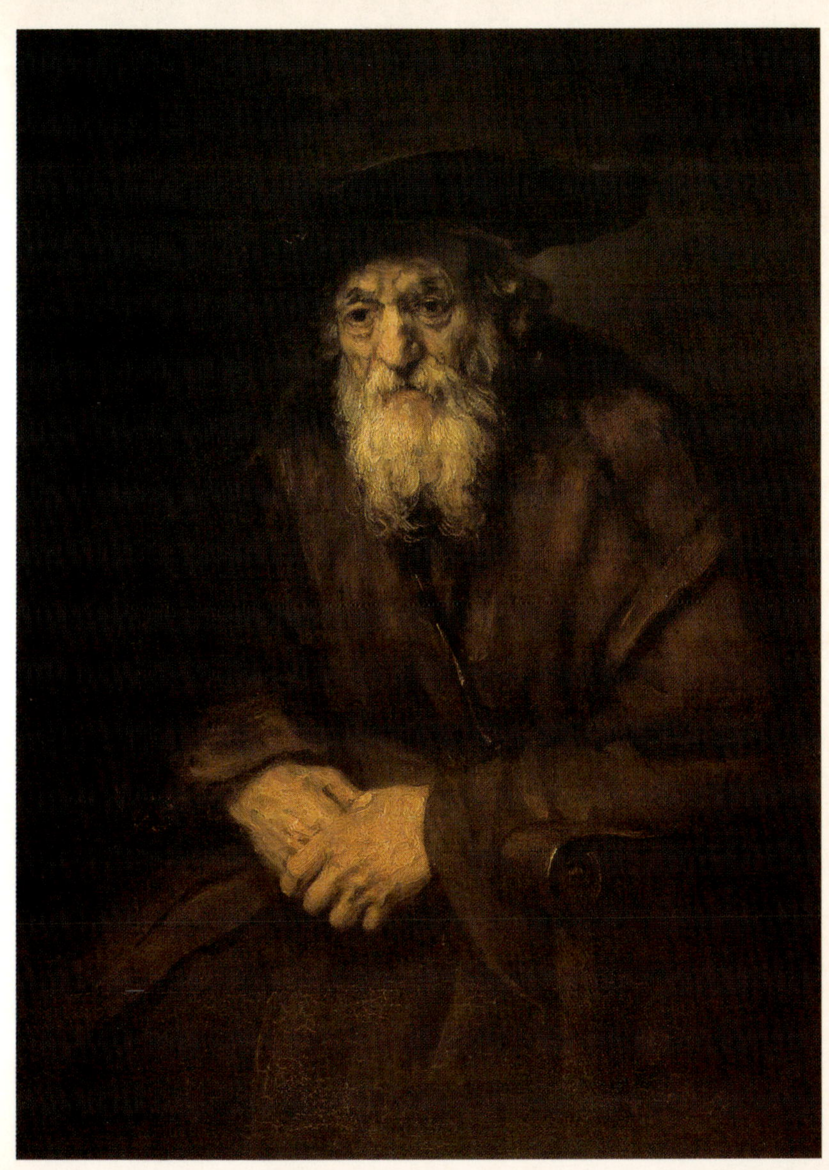

PORTRAIT OF AN OLD JEW, 1654
Oil on canvas. 109 x 84,8 cm
St. Petersburg, Hermitage Museum

PORTRAIT DE VIEUX JUIF, 1654
Huile sur toile. 109 x 84,8 cm
Saint-Pétersbourg, Musée de l'Ermitage

BILDNIS EINES ALTEN JUDEN, 1654
Öl auf Leinwand. 109 x 84,8 cm
St. Petersburg, Ermitage

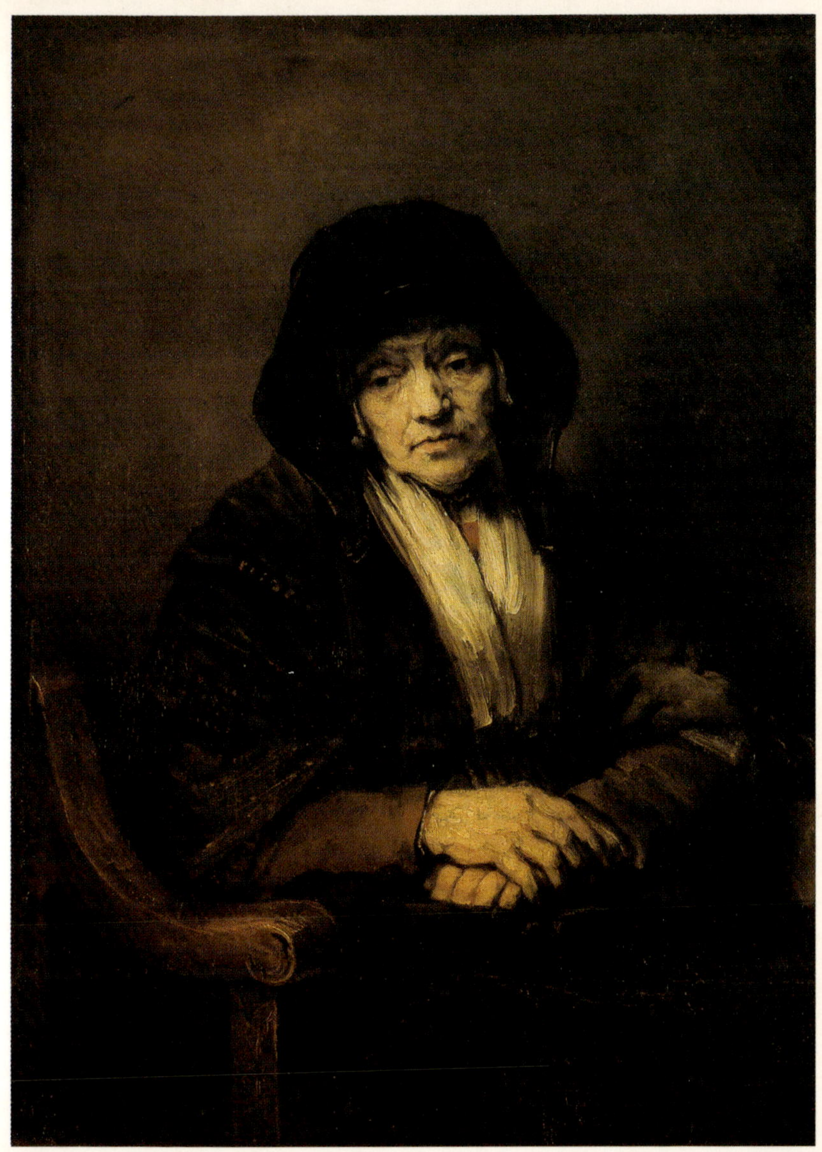

PORTRAIT OF AN OLD LADY, 1654
Oil on canvas. 109 x 84,5 cm
St. Petersburg, Hermitage Museum

PORTRAIT DE VIEILLE FEMME, 1654
Huile sur toile. 109 x 84,5 cm
Saint-Pétersbourg, Musée de l'Ermitage

BILDNIS EINER ALTER FRAU, 1654
Öl auf Leinwand. 109 x 84,5 cm
St. Petersburg, Ermitage

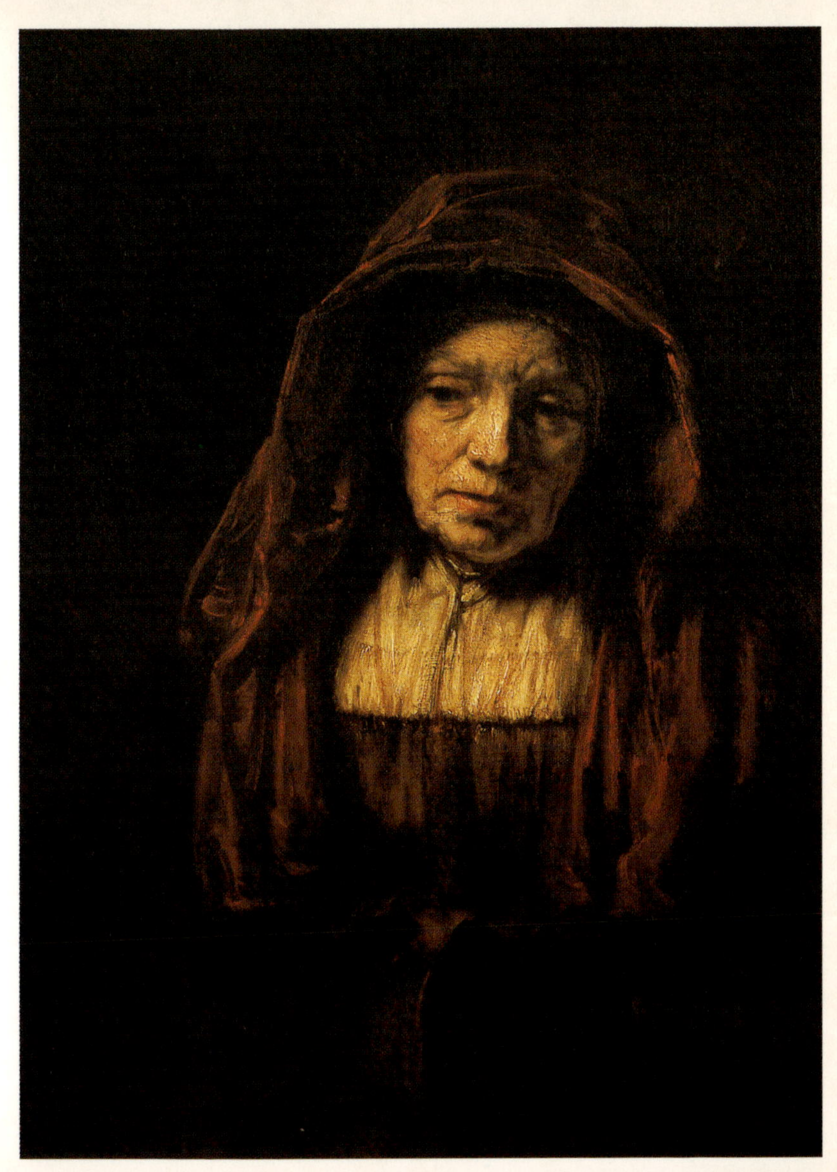

PORTRAIT OF AN OLD LADY, 1654
Oil on canvas. 74 x 63 cm
Moscow, Pushkin Museum

PORTRAIT DE VIEILLE FEMME, 1654
Huile sur toile. 74 x 63 cm
Moscou, Musée des Beaux Arts Pouchkine

BILDNIS EINER ALTER FRAU, 1654
Öl auf Leinwand. 74 x 63 cm
Moskau, Kunstmuseum Puschkin

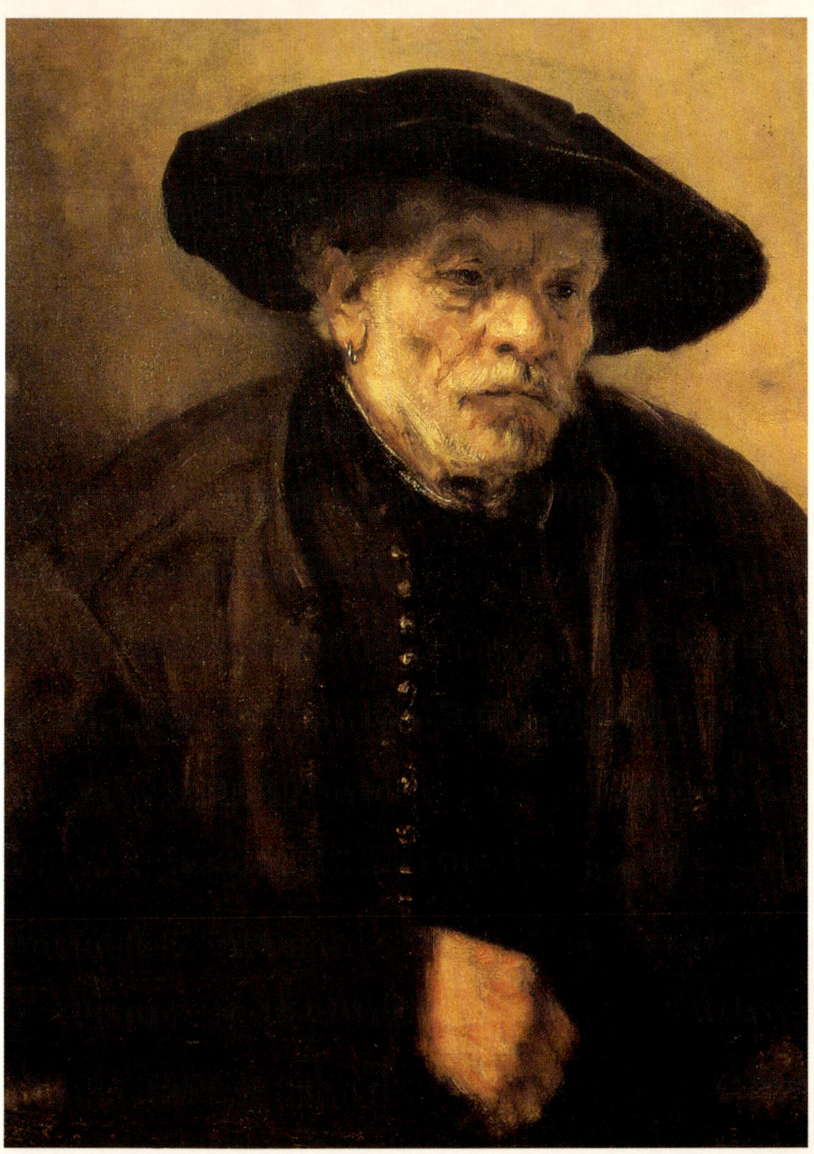

PORTRAIT OF ADRIAEN VAN RIJN,
THE ARTIST'S BROTHER (?), 1654
Oil on canvas. 74 x 63 cm
Moscow, Pushkin Museum

PORTRAIT D'ADRIAEN VAN RIJN,
FRERE DE L'ARTISTE (?), 1654
Huile sur toile. 74 x 63 cm
Moscou, Musée des Beaux Arts Pouchkine

BILDNIS ADRIAEN VAN RIJN,
BRUDER DES KÜNSTLERS (?), 1654
Öl auf Leinwand. 74 x 63 cm
Moskau, Kunstmuseum Puschkin

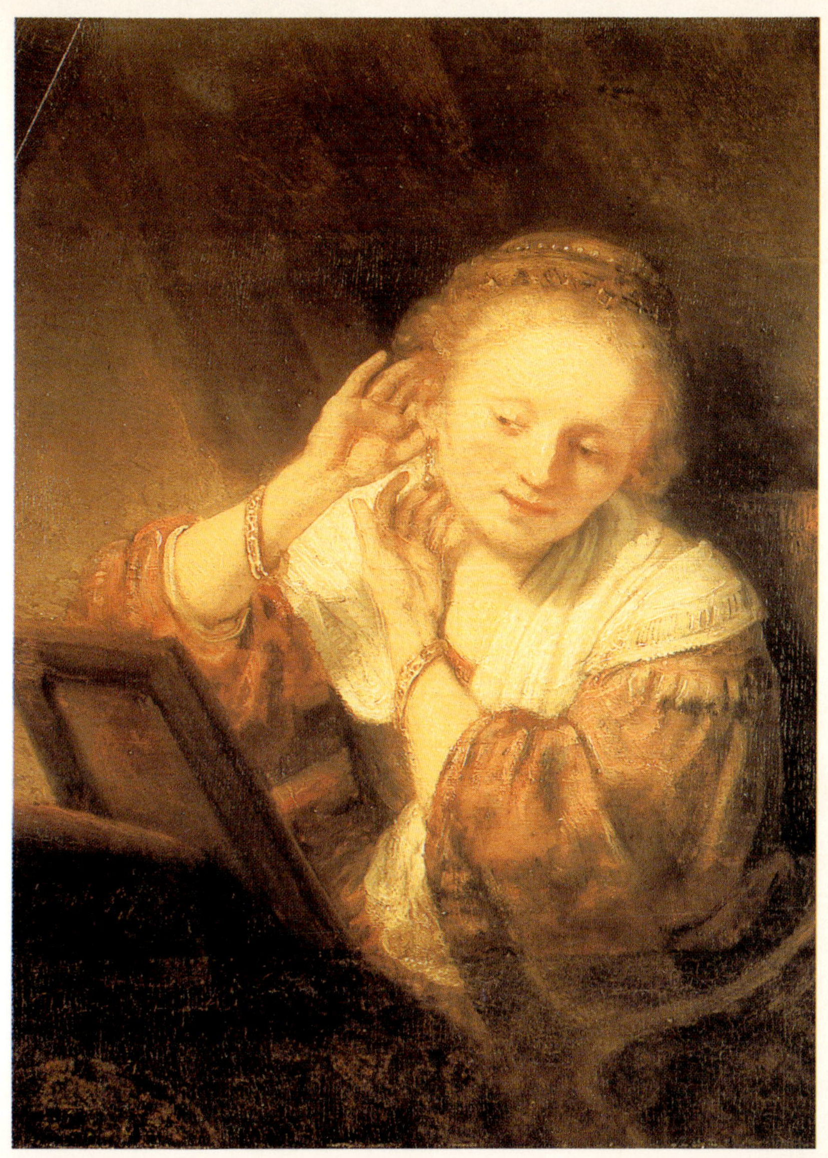

YOUNG LADY TRYING ON EARRINGS, 1657
Oil on wood. 39,5 x 32,5 cm
St. Petersburg, Hermitage Museum

JEUNE FEMME ESSAYANT DES BOUCLES
D'OREILLES, 1657
Huile sur bois. 39,5 x 32,5 cm
Saint-Pétersbourg, Musée de l'Ermitage

JUNGE FRAU, OHRRINGE ANPASSEND, 1657
Öl auf Holz. 39,5 x 32,5 cm
St. Petersburg, Ermitage

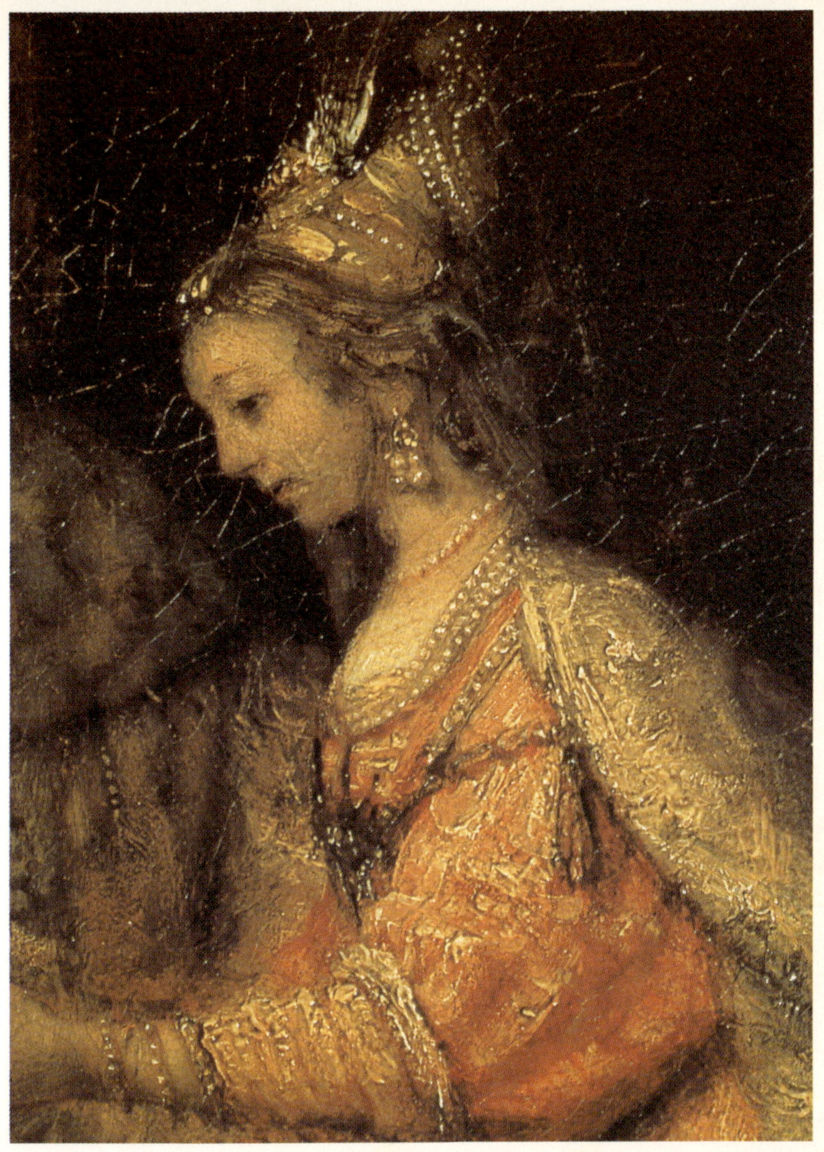

HAMAN AND AHASUERUS AT THE FEAST OF
ESTHER (Detail), 1660
Oil on canvas. 73 x 94 cm
Moscow, Pushkin Museum

AMAN, ESTHER ET ASSUERUS (Détail), 1660
Huile sur toile. 73 x 94 cm
Moscou, Musée des Beaux Arts Pouchkine

HAMAN, ESTHER UND AHASVERUS (Detail), 1660
Öl auf Leinwand. 73 x 94 cm
Moskau, Kunstmuseum Puschkin

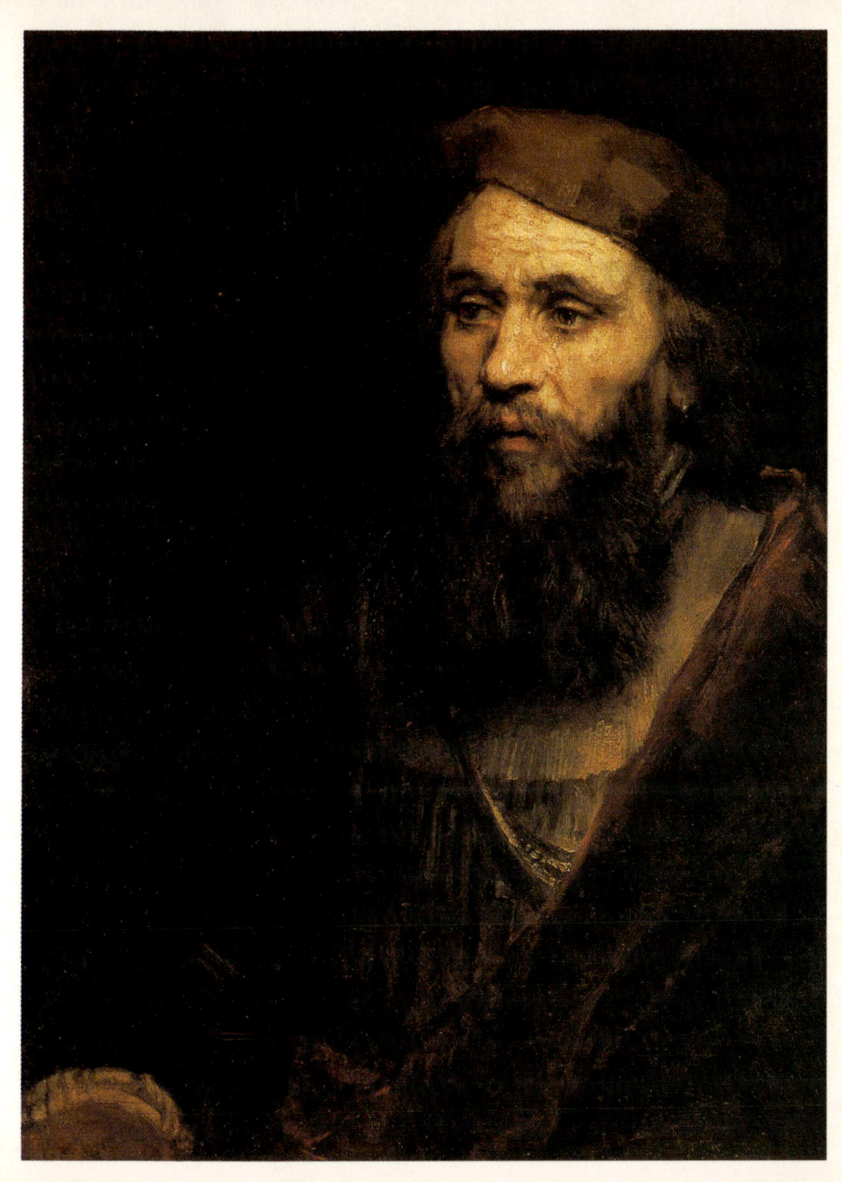

A BEARDED MAN, 1661
Oil on canvas. 71 x 61 cm
St. Petersburg, Hermitage Museum

PORTRAIT D'HOMME, 1661
Huile sur toile. 71 x 61 cm
Saint-Pétersbourg, Musée de l'Ermitage

MÄNNERBILDNIS, 1661
Öl auf Leinwand. 71 x 61 cm
St. Petersburg, Ermitage

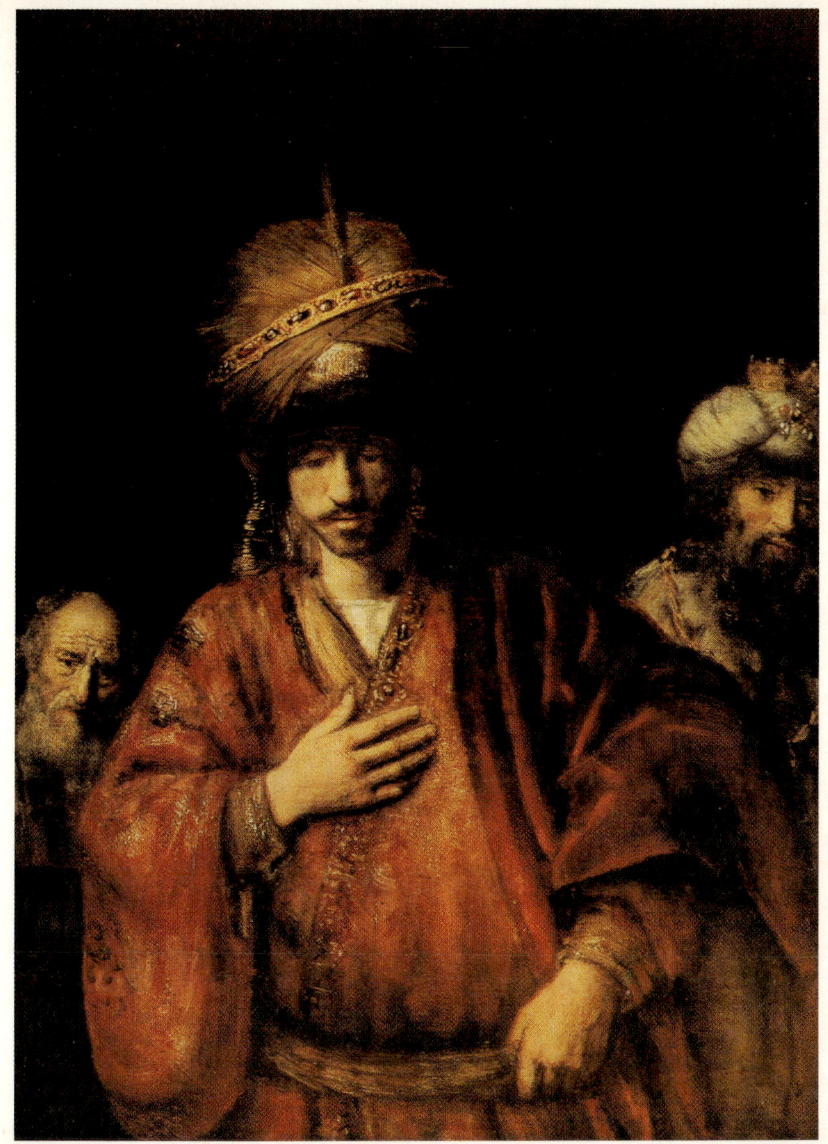

DAVID AND URIE (?)
Oil on canvas. 127 x 116 cm
St. Petersburg, Hermitage Museum

DAVID ET URIAH (?)
Huile sur toile. 127 x 116 cm
Saint-Pétersbourg, Musée de l'Ermitage

DAVID UND URIA (?)
Öl auf Leinwand. 127 x 116 cm
St. Petersburg, Ermitage

THE POET JEREMIAH DE DECKER, 1666
Oil on wood (oak). 71 x 56 cm
St. Petersburg, Hermitage Museum

PORTRAIT DU POÈTE JEREMIAS DE DECKER, 1666
Huile sur bois (chêne). 71 x 56 cm
Saint-Pétersbourg, Musée de l'Ermitage

BILDNIS DES DICHTERS JEREMIAS VAN DECKER, 1666
Öl auf Holz (eiche). 71 x 56 cm
St. Petersburg, Ermitage